I0479747

BUSINESS PRESENTATIONS START TO FINISH

A Practical Manual for Would-Be Presenters to Create and Deliver Outstanding Speeches at Work

Steven D. Nelson

ISBN: 9781650028477

To Marilyn Russell and Paul Nelson for all their support over the years, and to the amazing professors who have inspired me, especially Prof. John Kramer and Prof. Erica Benner. I also thank the many people I've coached over the years, who have shared their insights on presenting with me and given me the confidence to write this book.

CONTENTS

BUSINESS PRESENTATIONS START TO FINISH

HOW TO USE
THIS BOOK

"Jerrod, I'd like for you to give a status report on this project you're working on to the directors in New York. Do you think you can do that for the remote call next Thursday?"

"Uh, sure thing, boss!" (*gulp*)

YIKES! You have to give a presentation at work! Among the people I work with, there is almost nothing more stress-inducing than having to deliver a business presentation. Workers who are otherwise quite competent and self-assured can often become quivering jelly just contemplating the thought, even if they've done it many times before. And if English is not your first language, which is also the case with many of those I work with, then there is an extra layer of stress to deal with.

NOT TO WORRY. In this short book, I'll share with you the advice I've given to hundreds of business people on effective techniques for presenting your ideas at work, as well as things I've learned from training and coaching them over the years on this topic.

This book is designed to be a practical manual for busy professionals on how to design and create a stellar presentation, how to refine it into an effective way to communicate your message, and how to deliver it in the most memorable and impressive manner. It isn't intended to be the most comprehensive discussion of this wide-ranging topic, but rather a compact guide to give you the practical skills needed for dynamic presentations, and possibly loosen any resistance you might have towards presenting.

For many of you, there will undoubtedly be information in this book that you've heard before. Repetition can be very useful, as we will talk about later. My experience is that we all know many workable ideas, but we do not put them into action until we hear them repeated more than once. And it can be very beneficial to hear a familiar concept presented with a new perspective, or framed in a different way than what we've heard in the past.

In addition, you may also not read this book from cover to cover, but rather focus more on specific areas related to presenting. If this is the case for you, feel free to go straight to sections that you think you need to work on most and just look up the information presented there.

However you decide to consume the information in this book, there is one essential point to keep in mind. You can read and learn as much as possible about giving presentations, or watch videos of great speakers and try to take apart their speeches to figure out what makes them amazing. And you should!

None of that, however, will make you into a great presenter by itself. As I tell my clients, there is only one way to become truly great: *by giving presentations!* All of the information in the world on its own will not make you a better presenter. We only get better at business skills by actually practicing them.

Even then, just practicing the skill is the absolute minimum. Ideally, the best way of improving your skills is through following this simple and straightforward loop:

- apply best practices techniques in your business presentations
- get as much helpful and constructive feedback as you can
- adjust your presentations based on the feedback you get, and try it again

Following this advice, with the right amount of practice and feedback, I believe anyone is capable of delivering outstanding presentations at work. I've seen amazing transformations over the years of shy and insecure speakers who have become confident, powerful presenters, able to command an entire room of people.

Just don't forget that everything you learn in this book is meant to be applied in the real world. I would love to hear how this material has affected you and what you've learned from it, so please drop me an email at steven@stevendnelson.com to share your ideas, reflections, and stories of success, and leave a review of this book online so others can learn about it too.

STARTING OFF

B efore we learn how to create a business presentation, it's useful to first discuss what we actually mean by one and in what kinds of situations we can apply the information presented here. We'll also take a look at how to cope with the fear that frequently accompanies having to present in front of others.

What do we consider to be a business presentation?

For most people, the phrase "business presentation" probably conjures up a specific image: one of a single person or a small group of people, standing in front of a larger group of seated audience members, while talking on a given topic as they advance a slideshow displayed behind them. This is certainly one type of presentation, but not the only one in which you may put your presentational skills to use.

In the context of this book, "business" simply means "work-related," so it covers any type of presentational structure that you have to give at work or in relation to your job. What can this mean? Here are some possible situations in which you may have to use your presentational skills at work:

- updating senior managers on a conference call about the status of your latest project
- informing your team members on your plans for the day at a morning stand-up meeting
- giving a demonstration to new employees on proper safety procedures
- holding an informal discussion with company interns on what expectations the company has of them
- explaining a complicated procedure to a colleague on the phone
- presenting a detailed project proposal to your manager in a private meeting

The topics covered in this book can help you deliver your message more effectively for each of these situations.

We'll consider a "business presentation" as simply "a situation in which a worker speaks on a specific, work-related topic for at least a few minutes." This situation can also include discussion with the audience, as strong presenters do not communicate on a one-way basis only but also encourage interaction with their audience.

In the interest of simplicity, a standing talk in front of a group of people with a slideshow will serve as the default model of a "business presentation" as we examine best practices for every element of it. If you regularly give a different type of work-related presentation, you may only need to apply the parts of this book that are relevant to that kind of presentation.

Dealing with stage fright

Many people dislike giving presentations or any type of public speaking because of the pressure and anxiety it creates, as with Jerrod from the introduction. If this is you, you can take comfort in knowing that you're not alone in this.

And naturally, the anxiety level increases when you have your colleagues and possibly supervisors watching you. You may even feel that your future career is on the line if you don't do a good job with it.

But I encourage you not to think this way. I would actually turn this thinking around and argue that your future career is on the line if you *avoid* giving presentations, or if you don't put any effort into improving your skills in this area. Employees who decide not to develop their presentation skills will find their job opportunities severely limited in a white-collar setting.

This point is underlined by a conversation I once had with the head of a fairly large company. As I happened to be walking by his office, he stopped me and asked about one of his managers who had attended a training workshop of mine. The CEO confided in me during this conversation that this manager's presentation skills were not as strong as they should be for someone at his level. This comment gave me the impression that his manager would not be going any higher in his career until he improves his ability in this area.

For the sake of your job and future career opportunities, it is well worth putting in the effort to overcome your fears and make an effort to become a better presenter. But telling yourself you should overcome your fear of presenting is one thing, and actually doing it is another. How *do* we do it?

First of all, we should consider why people experience anxiety when they have to give a speech in front of others. They feel this anxiety acutely when they become aware of others focusing their full attention towards them, and they get unnerved to see many people watching them at once.

We can say that having stage fright is a form of heightened self-consciousness, when we get nervous and uncomfortable because we are overly concerned about what people think about us or our behavior. In other words, a phobia of speaking publicly is rooted in a fear that is inward focused. All sorts of "me-centered" questions occupy our brains at this time: *Am I doing this right? Do I look okay? What do they think about me? What if I say the wrong thing or mess something up?* And so on.

It's completely fine to be nervous about giving a presentation, and I would say it's even a healthy response to the situation. As we will see a bit later, speaking in front of others is not a natural state for most of us, and it requires behaving in a way that often feels uncomfortable because we're not used to it.

A feeling of apprehension and nervousness can even be interpreted as a sign that you are taking the presentation seriously and want to give it your best. Conversely, if you appear overly relaxed to your audience, you might come off to them as ambivalent about your topic, and unconcerned whether your message gets through to them or not.

So experiencing anxiety and feeling nervous before and during a presentation is not in and of itself a problem, but rather when it is focused too much on ourselves. What you should do is take your nervous energy and focus it outside yourself instead of inside. Admittedly, this is easy to say and hard to put into practice when the pressure's on. But try taking these steps when you feel overwhelmed by presenter's fright:

- Try not to concentrate on "me-centered" questions like, "How do I look to the audience?" (solution: check yourself before the presentation in the restroom mirror until you feel comfortable with your appearance), or "Am I doing a good job of conveying my message?" (solution: trust in yourself and the preparation you've done beforehand).
- Channel your focus outward, directing it toward the audience. Imagine that the nervous energy you feel inside is passing through you to your listeners by way of your voice, your gestures, your eyes, and your body, and it is assisting you in communicating your message. Be energized by the thought of offering useful information to the audience and how they will be able to benefit from it.
- Don't get overwhelmed when you notice everyone in the audience observing you at once. Remind yourself that the audience is on your side and genuinely wants your presentation to succeed. They will be forgiving of any mistakes you make in your presentation delivery if they can see that you are truly making an effort.
- Accept and embrace any anxiety and nervousness you feel, and know that it is just part of the process of becoming comfortable with presenting. The more presentations you give, the easier it will get over time as you become used to speaking in front

of others.

Now that we've looked at what kind of situations can be considered business presentations and how to overcome the fears associated with them, we'll next examine how to construct one from scratch.

RECAP:

- Business presentations can cover many types of situations when you have to present an idea at work. Apply the necessary information in this book to the kind of presentation you regularly give.

- When dealing with stage fright, embrace your anxiety and try to focus it outward towards your audience as energy that will help you convey your topic.

- Don't get overly concerned with "me-centered" questions, but instead concentrate on giving the audience a fantastic experience with your performance.

FINDING YOUR PURPOSE

Have you ever had the experience of sitting in a confusing presentation and thinking: *What is the point of all this? Why is this person telling me this information?* I have had that unfulfilling feeling many times, and it happens because the presenter was likely not clear on this point themselves. So the first thing you need to determine is the reason *why* you are giving the presentation. What is it you want to achieve with your talk? Even if it seems self-evident to you, spell it out in writing.

You might think that it's unnecessary in some cases. When you're told, "Share the results of your report to the big boss," the task seems straightforward enough, and so there's no need to specify a purpose. All you have to do is gather the necessary information and write your speech, right?

Not so fast! It's worth taking the time, even for presentations that seem to have obvious objectives, to be *very, very clear* about your purpose for giving them. Let's take a look at why that is and how to do it.

Every presentation needs to have an *overall purpose* and a *specific message*. Public speeches can have several types of overall purposes, but there are essentially only two for the majority of business presentations: *informational* and *persuasive*.

This means that for nearly every single business presentation, you are either *attempting to transfer information on a specific topic to others* (informational), or *urging them to take some type of action* (persuasive). For most companies, one of these two purposes comprise nearly all of their presentations.

Be clear about your overall purpose first. Suppose you have to give a presentation on hazard prevention in the workplace to company employees. Is the point of the talk simply to tell the audience about the topic so that they know what action to take in certain situations, such as when spills in the kitchen occur (informational), or is the point of the presentation to get them to take specific action, like preventing repetitive strain injuries at their desks or keeping areas of high traffic clear of obstacles (persuasive)? Find out for sure if you are not completely certain.

Once you know whether you are delivering an informational or persuasive speech, you then need to determine your presentation's *specific message*, which we'll simply call your "message" from this point on. Your message is particular to each presentation you give, meaning every presentation you deliver should have its own distinct message.

In essence, your message is simply the answer to the question, *What do I want my audience to think or do differently after the presentation?* You should think in terms of a transformation: the kind of change you want to cause in the audience to either make them think about something differently or cause them to do something.

There can only be one answer to this question, even if you give a long presentation, and you should be able to write it down in a single sentence. If you can't do that, your presentation will lack a clear focus and be muddled.

Your message gives you a basis on which to build up your presentation, which is why you have to come up with it first. Everything in your speech flows from your message and needs to be related to it. Anything in your speech not directly related to this purpose should not be in your speech at all.

Oftentimes presenters stray from their message and go off on a tangential point. If they spend too much time on this point, it becomes the main focus of the speech, and the audience starts to think thoughts like, "Wait, I thought this presentation was about how we can retain high-performing employees, but now it seems to be a list of reasons why high performers get dissatisfied and leave. Which one is it about, the first or the second?" You never want to confuse your audience in this way.

The audience can forgive most mistakes made by a presenter. Nearly everyone gets nervous speaking in front of others, especially when talking to a large number of people or to VIPs. If you have compelling content, the audience is willing to overlook your imperfect delivery up to a point.

But the audience is less forgiving if you are not clear with your message. It makes them have to focus on figuring out what it is that you are trying to communicate rather than evaluating your ideas. Worse, an unclear purpose also indicates to the audience that you did not devote enough time to preparation before getting up to speak.

Ideally, your message should avoid generalities and contain details. The more detailed it is, the easier it will be to construct a talk around it. You should also attempt to tailor your message to the needs and interests of your audience, as we'll learn more about in a later chapter.

For example, let's say you have an informational presentation and you've decided your message is "to explain recent changes in procurement procedures." This message is workable in its current state, but we can still improve it. Ask yourself these questions: *Are there some changes that are more significant than others? Which ones are particularly relevant to the people you'll be addressing? How deeply do you plan to explain the changes?* The answers to these questions will help you refine your message and give it a stronger focus.

A better message statement for this example might be, "to give a detailed overview of recent changes in the company's procurement procedures, particularly how they affect major purchases." This statement also informs how you will be able to structure your presentation, which we'll look at in the next section.

RECAP:

- Most business presentations have an overall purpose that is designed either to inform or persuade others. Make sure you are clear about which one your presentation is supposed to do first.

- Create a specific message for your presentation, which simply answers: *What do I want my audience to think or do differently after the presentation?* This should be stated in one sentence, and it will be the main focus of your presentation.

- Refine your message by making it detailed and also by tailoring it to the audience you are presenting to.

CREATING STRUCTURE

Once you have decided upon a message for your presentation, the next step is to develop a structure around your thoughts and ideas. But we first need to examine one of the most crucial elements in a presentation: the presenter's relationship with their audience.

Addressing the audience's needs and interests

For every type of public speaking, there is an unspoken "social contract" between the presenter and their audience. When a presenter begins to speak before an audience, the audience essentially agrees to give their time and attention to that presenter. But in return, *the audience expects the speaker to give them something of value in return for their time and attention.* This is what I consider the "social contract" of public speaking.

Looked at another way, we presenters have been given an incredible gift when we speak: a captive audience that pays attention to us! And we should always keep in mind that, according to the "terms" of this contract, our obligation to the audience is to address their needs and interests, which we then frame our ideas around.

When you don't put the audience's needs and interests foremost in your presentation, or even worse, disregard them completely, the audience feels cheated. After all, they are fulfilling their side of this agreement by giving you their time and paying attention, but you are not upholding your side of the bargain. This invariably results in an audience feeling dissatisfied.

It is even more critical if there are senior managers present. As their time and attention is what they value most, they will not appreciate it if you use it unwisely by not giving them value in your presentation. You provide value to them by addressing their needs and interests.

But you can only speak to your audience's needs and interests if you know something about them. So learn as much as you can about your prospective audience before you present to them.

This likely doesn't pose a problem when giving presentations to just your team or your direct manager. You probably already know what these people want to hear, and in many cases their interests also coincide with your own. But don't assume that employees in other departments always have the same interests as you, or that managers that you don't have close contact with are necessarily interested in the same things that your direct manager is.

Recently, one of my students, James, had to prepare for a visit from a senior manager to his office. She had asked him, among other things, to prepare a 5-minute presentation on the current project he was working on. James felt at a loss at how to approach this task, not to mention nervous at the thought of presenting in front of such a high-powered individual, whom he had never presented in front of before.

I encouraged James to ask around and find out what kind of information she wanted to hear and how she preferred to have it presented to her. Following this, he found out that she valued broad overviews over technical details, and that she was primarily interested in how his work contributed to the company as a whole. This insight provided James with a starting point that he could confidently build a presentation structure around.

The basic structure of a great business presentation

Humans have been speculating about the right way to craft a public speech since at least ancient Greece, when Aristotle discussed this topic in his treatise "Rhetoric." But perhaps one of the best-known formulas for structuring a speech is a short and memorable statement, created much later, that has been ascribed to various persons over the years. You have likely heard it before:

Tell the audience what you're going to say, say it, then tell them what you've said.

I'm generally a fan of simplicity wherever possible, and I think this catchy phrase is an excellent summarization of how to create a business presentation structure, though I would expand it in a few important ways. Below is my five-step formula for developing your own presentation.

Five steps to an effective business presentation structure:

1. Use an opening that grabs the listener's attention
2. Outline the content of your presentation, and indicate why it is important to the audience
3. Present your main points, and connect each point to the needs and interests of your audience
4. Provide a summary of your main points and their benefits to the audience
5. Finish with your main takeaway – what you want the audience to remember after they leave

Let's take a detailed look at each of these steps.

Use an opening that grabs the listener's attention

The audience is particularly receptive to your message at the beginning of the presentation. They generally have a high amount of interest and attention at the start of your talk, meaning the first 30-60 seconds after you begin speaking. After this point, the audience's attention naturally wanes unless you do something to draw them in through compelling content and delivery.

A strong start pulls the audience in from the first thing you say. Consider the differences between these two possible presentation openings and the advantages and drawbacks of each one:

> *"Nice to see you all here today. As most of you know, my name is Dwayne Myers and I'm going to talk about how we can use effective time management techniques to boost our productivity at work."*

> *"Hi everyone. We all know how precious our time is,*

and we understand the need to use it in the best way possible when we're at work. In this presentation, I'm going to give you the knowledge you need to make the most out of the hours in your workday."

The first opening statement is pretty standard. It is more or less the way most of us are accustomed to opening a business presentation, or how we think we need to open one. It follows a familiar pattern:

friendly greeting → *personal introduction* → *topic statement*

The advantage of this opening is that it covers the bases in terms of who the speaker is, if not known to the audience, and a statement that outlines what the presentation will be about. It isn't terrible – and in fact, making clear who you are and what you're going to talk about is useful information for the audience to know.

The disadvantage of this opening is that it doesn't grab the audience and draw them into your message in a compelling way. You have set expectations as, "This is a standard business presentation, much like many others I've heard in the past."

But here's the thing about opening a business presentation: you don't have to do it in any "standard" way, or the same way you have seen it done in other presentations. In fact, opening a presentation it in a non-traditional way instantly sets you apart and makes you more memorable from other speakers.

Now let's examine the second opening. This one follows a more non-traditional pattern:

short greeting → *general factual statement* → *hook*
(value proposition)

In contrast to the first opening, this one starts in a way that the listener doesn't expect. It jumps straight into a statement that many of us would find hard to disagree with (the value of time and the need to use it effectively), following up with a promise to provide value to the listener.

This opening statement draws the audience in and makes them feel as if the information they're about to hear will be interesting and useful. Even listeners who may not even care about time management at all will be intrigued by this unorthodox beginning and direct appeal to their interests.

Note that the second opening does not include an introduction, meaning a statement that says who you are, where you work, or your authority on the topic. Obviously, this is unnecessary if your audience is already familiar with you (such as presentations delivered to your team), but with listeners who do not know you yet, you may feel a strong need to introduce yourself.

In such cases, I recommend getting another person to introduce you before you speak. This frees you up to jump right into your topic and focus the audience's attention on your message. In addition, there is an added bit of credibility imparted upon you when another person introduces you in front of a group of people.

If there's no one already arranged to introduce you, ask someone assisting with the presentation in an organizational role, perhaps a meeting facilitator or host, to give a short introduction for you. If you're not used to asking others to do this for you, don't be shy! It is unlikely that any host or organizer will decline your request for an introduction.

The main sticking point for them is likely to be that they simply won't know what to say in your introduction. They may also think of composing an introduction as yet another task that they have to do on top of everything else.

So here's what you can do: before someone introduces you as a presenter, write out your own introduction and hand it to them. A hard copy of your introduction is probably best. You can also send it to them electronically, but make sure you have a hard copy on hand when you arrive in person. When you start your presentation, you don't need to repeat any information already stated in the introduction, but it is acceptable to thank the person who introduced you.

You may also feel it necessary in your opening statement to state your authority on the presentation topic. Preferably, the person introducing you should do this so you don't have to. If no one introduces you, then combine any statement on your qualifications on the topic together with the benefits they offer to the audience. For example, "Time management has been one of my personal interests for years, and a topic that I've conducted extensive research on. This presentation will distill the main takeaways I've learned."

However you decide to open your presentation, remember you should *start strong*. A strong start is one that's memorable, resonates with your message, and draws the audience into your speech. Here are a few other ways to open your presentation that can grab the audience's attention if done correctly:

- surprising fact or statistic ("A recent study found that a 20% of an average employee's time at work is taken up by unnecessary tasks that could easily be eliminated.")
- personal anecdote ("A few years ago I thought about why I was never able to leave work before 6 pm. I then became determined to use my time more efficiently so I wouldn't have to stay later than my normal working hours every day.")
- personalized rhetorical question ("Have you ever thought about how to get more things done at work during the same amount of time?")
- general rhetorical question ("What's the best way to make employees feel that their time is valued while at work? If you thought, 'managing their time better,' you would be right.")

The idea is to open your presentation in an unexpected way that still connects with the message you are trying to communicate. Many people think that a good way to open a presentation is to tell a joke, as humor gets the audience's attention by creating a laugh and lightening up the mood.

I'll address the general use of humor in presentations in a later chapter, but regarding its use in openings, I generally don't recommend starting your business presentations this way. Mostly this is because even though a joke may get the audience's attention, it often doesn't relate to your message. And anything in your presentation that does not resonate with or support the message of your presentation will detract from it.

What's more, you might want to think about what would happen if your joke bombs with the audience! This can occur even with jokes that you have told before in similar settings, or with the same presentation to a different audience. If this happens, you have now started your presentation in a very awkward way that will be hard to recover from. You could undermine your credibility and the professional image you want to project, depending on how the joke is received.

This is not to say that you should avoid humor completely in your presentation, as it can certainly be a great way to keep the audience's interest and attention during your speech. I just don't think you should open a presentation this way.

Outline the content of your presentation, and indicate why it is important to the audience

This step is comparable to the "tell the audience what you're going to say" part. But it also includes the benefits that the audience will receive, ensuring that the audience remains engaged in your message.

Why is it important to outline the content of your presentation? One metaphor I find useful in thinking about presentations is comparing the presenter to the role of a tour guide and the audience as tourists. We are taking our audience on a kind of journey that we know well, but it is unknown to them. Since the audience doesn't know where we're taking them, we reassure them by informing them what we're going to "see" on this trip through our presentation.

Outlining the content of your presentation does not have to be long or complicated. In fact, the more concise you make your outline, the easier it is for your audience to understand where they're going on this journey that you're taking them on. For the time management topic above, you could say:

> *"First we're going to take a look some of the unexpected things that tend to decrease worker productivity in our industry. Then we'll examine some of the roots of these barriers to greater productivity and how they can be overcome. Finally, I'll give you a list of specific actionable steps our company can take that will have a measurable impact on improving worker productivity, which, as we know, the board has set as a major objective for the upcoming year."*

Your outline can also be longer or shorter than this. However long it is, you need to tell the audience what information they're going to hear, which direction it's going to go in, and how it's going to end up.

You should also include a statement that indicates *why* your presentation is important to the audience. This is achieved by the last phrase in this example outline above, *"which, as we know, the board has set as a major objective for the upcoming year."* This is the "clincher" for the outline, telling the audience why they should care about your speech. It "sells" your presentation to the audience and reminds them why their time and attention is worth devoting to you.

Note that the "clincher" statement does not have to be something completely new or unfamiliar to the audience. I often tell my clients not to be afraid to "state the obvious" by saying something already familiar to those listening. It works as long as you can connect it to your message.

For a presentation, say, about a new process for handling customer complaints, you could point out the problems and struggles with the current procedure, even if you know everyone present is already well aware that they exist. In this way, you remind the audience of the relevance of your presentation and position your idea as the way to overcome that problem.

Present your main points, and connect each point to the needs and interests of your audience

This is the part of your presentation where you expand on your message and build evidence for it so that, by the end, the audience thinks about something in a new or different way, or takes some action. You set out the main points of your message and develop them through various rhetorical techniques. It is the most substantial part of your presentation and generally takes up most of your speaking time.

It may also help to think about your presentation as analogous to a tree. Your message is the tree trunk – strong and deeply rooted, but if weak, your tree will easily collapse. The main points that develop your message are like the branches of the tree. They emerge from the trunk and are all connected to it, and help the tree expand its width and scope. Let's take a look at some of the techniques that create strong branches for your presentation.

Add details
Details give specific information on the who, what, when, why, where, and how that relate to the main points of your presentation. To continue with the tree metaphor

for a moment, we can think of the details of your speech as the tree's leaves. Leaves make a tree interesting and appealing due to the way they flutter and reflect sunlight. Without leaves, a tree is not very beautiful. We call it "bare," or uninteresting.

Details serve the same function in your presentation. The specific details you state in your presentation distinguish it from every other presentation on that topic. They also make your presentation memorable, as the audience is likely to remember the specifics contained in your speech.

I'm always disappointed when I watch presentations or other kinds of public speeches that lack details. It seems to me that the speaker has omitted the most interesting parts of the presentation – what makes it unique. They've given a speech that anyone could make on this particular topic.

What kind of details should you include in our presentation? The best details are ones that give color to your stories and illustrate the points that serve your message. Details also let you tailor your message to the particular audience you're addressing.

Use examples to ground your message

Examples are powerful because they translate your message from theory into practice. This is particularly key for business presentations because of the need for practicality in business. Your business presentation, in other words, is not the place to ruminate on philosophical concepts. Examples keep your message grounded in the business world.

Use examples selectively but powerfully – you want to highlight the points that contribute to your message. For persuasive presentations, the most powerful examples typically come from stories of other companies that have already implemented the ideas or concepts you are promoting. This is because of the power of "social proof," meaning that your idea appears more credible with the knowledge that another group of business people has already taken the risk to test it out before you do.

Suppose you want to convince your company to set aside a room in your office as a "mindfulness space," a place where employees can release the tension and stress of work in a quiet, uninterrupted environment. An example in your presentation could list other companies comparable to yours that have already dedicated such quiet rooms in their workplaces. It would be even more convincing if you repeated the employees' own words on how such places have helped their well-being, or quoted data demonstrating the beneficial effect on employee productivity that taking breaks in such a room provides.

Tell personal stories

You might think that your personal life is off limits in the office setting, and that a business presentation is not the appropriate venue to share stories about yourself. But this isn't the case! You can add interest and variety to your presentations through the effective use of personal stories.

Granted, there is less scope for personal stories in business presentations than in other types of public speaking. If you are giving a toast at a wedding or speaking at a funeral, for example, your *entire speech* might be composed of personal stories about the relevant persons at the event. But it would be out of place if we did the same thing in a business presentation.

In addition, you probably don't want to get *too* personal and offer details about your life that would be inappropriate to share in the workplace. Appropriate personal stories resonate with your message and support it. Your own experiences make your points in a unique way because the audience can relate to them personally. If done well, the audience can imagine themselves in your situation, making it easier for them to accept your message.

A participant in one of my workshops once told me that his manager asked him to create a presentation on an algorithm, which he thought would be a boring topic. He was at a complete loss, unable to figure out how to liven it up and make it interesting.

In response, I encouraged him to personalize the topic to make it appealing to the audience. One option I mentioned would be to frame the topic in terms of what his workflow was like before he started using the algorithm, and how it had changed as a result of applying it.

I also suggested he talk about the amount of time he had saved as a result of using this algorithm and how it had made his life easier, as well as cases of how it had helped others. By the end of the workshop, he had found a way to take a topic that he felt was drab and make it much more interesting by talking about his personal experiences.

Use expert sources

Have you ever noticed that a lot of books designed to teach you something often use quotations, usually from widely known people? They do this to draw upon the expertise and fame of the person making the quote to add support to their own argument.

Similarly, in your presentation you can also use the opinions and professional judgment of experts to provide additional support for your message. This adds extra legitimacy to your argument, as it is no longer just your own opinion you are expressing, but that of a credible and trusted source that appears to be on your side.

Expert sources may consist of either individuals with outstanding credentials, or organizations like government entities, research institutes, or universities. For organizations, you can present the findings of studies, reports, or surveys.

Here are some potential sources you can draw from to offer expert opinion:

- famous entrepreneurs or heads of current major companies
- individual experts recognized in your company's particular field or industry
- trade groups in your industry
- top management at your own company
- management experts in academia, especially those with well-known books on business

Use data and statistics

You may have heard the advice, "speak from the heart," meaning that you should use language and techniques to appeal to people's emotions, particularly when you give persuasive presentations. While it's true that people tend to make decisions based on emotion rather than logic, don't discount the benefits of hard data for business presentations.

This is because presentations given at work ultimately serve some type of business purpose that are expected to lead to a concrete, measurable bottom line result for the company. Thus, numbers play a greater role in business presentations than in other types of public speaking, and your presentation will most likely require some type of data and statistics to help you make your points.

Data and statistics provide objective information to expand your message outside of the realm of simply subjective opinion. You can also combine expert sources along with data to strengthen a particular point.

Think about the difference between these two statements below, and how the data in the second one reinforces the point and makes it more convincing and substantial (all information provided here is made up for this example):

> *"Many companies have already been targeted by various types of phishing scams, but the vast majority of firms still do not have any formal policies in place to handle suspicious emails or phone calls."*

> *"A recent survey by computer security specialists Smith and Smith estimates that 38% of American companies have been targeted by various types of phishing scams, but a surprising 70% of them still do not have any formal policies in place to handle suspicious emails or phone calls."*

The specificity of the concrete numbers by a credible source in the second statement greatly adds to the strength of your argument, especially in comparison to the vague wording in the first statement.

Provide a summary of
your main points and their
benefits to the audience

This is the "tell them what you've said" part of your presentation, when you briefly review the main points of your message, but you also restate the benefits of these points to your listeners. The summary serves two purposes: to stress the key parts of the message you want them to remember, and also remind them *why* these points are important to remember.

Why do you have to state again the benefits of your message in the summary? This reminds the audience that you understand and respect the "social contract" of public speaking that we discussed earlier, showing that you have kept your end of the bargain by offering them something valuable in return for the time and attention they've given you. Even if your message somehow fails to resonate with every person in your audience for some reason, they will still be able to appreciate your attempt to address their needs and interests.

In your summary, use a phrase that indicates you are going to review your main points, then go through these points one by one, tying them together in a final statement. Here's one way you could do it:

"To recap the key points from this talk, our current share of the domestic market is stable at 24% but has been stagnant for some time. The major factors that prevent us from increasing our market share are the weak economic environment and an aging product line. But our surveys with consumers show that revitalizing our product line and targeting different segments of the market could help us gain ground. If we implement these changes, we have a greater chance of reaching our targets for next year."

The final sentence of this example is key, as it highlights how your presentation relates to a measurable, bottom-line result for the company.

Finish with your main takeaway
– what you want the audience
to remember after they leave

Your audience may enjoy your presentation, and hopefully your style and message will resonate with them. But what will they recall of your presentation an hour after you've finished? How about the next day? Two weeks later? A month? A year? Will they remember anything at all about it by that point?

Granted, not every business presentation needs to be remembered long afterwards. A presentation on the weekly sales data, for example, will probably be mostly forgotten by the next week, and rightly so. But even for presentations with a lower shelf life than others, a takeaway statement is a great way to crystalize your message into a useful sound bite to leave for the audience.

You can in fact create and implant a statement in your listeners' minds that will remain with them long after your presentation is over. Whatever this is should reflect your message in some way.

Think about one specific thing that you want your audience to remember about your presentation even if they forget everything else. It should be a single line that is closely related to your message. Close your presentation with that line, as people tend to remember best the last thing they hear. Deliver it with the importance it deserves.

You can also reinforce the takeaway statement by putting it on your last slide. Since most people take questions after their presentation, your last slide is typically the most important one, as it is usually on the screen the longest.

But despite its importance, what do the majority of final slides have written on them? Usually it's phrases like "Q&A," "Questions?" "Thank you for your attention," and so forth. It's these phrases that will be on the screen as you take questions from the audience, and unfortunately these phrases will be the ones in their minds when they go back to work after your presentation.

So instead of phrases like "Thank you!" or "Q&A" on your last slide, which may be polite and functional but do not reflect your message, put your takeaway statement on the last slide instead. This is how you ensure that this thought is foremost in the audience's mind as you wrap up your talk.

It's worth pointing out that you can craft a decent presentation from just following Steps 2, 3 and 4. These three steps are essentially the "Tell the audience what you're going to say, say it, then tell them what you've said" formulation, with an emphasis on how this information is relevant and beneficial to your particular audience. Any presentation with only these three elements will have a satisfactory presentation structure.

But including Steps 1 and 5 as well makes for a truly memorable experience. Starting the presentation with an opening that grabs the audience's attention pulls the audience into your message by taking advantage of their heightened interest at the start of the talk. Likewise, closing with a distilled form of your message in a takeaway statement leaves the audience with the most important thing you want them to remember.

These two extra steps, taken together, also frame your talk in a way that is satisfying to the audience, in that the opening identifies a particular topic or issue, while the takeaway resolves it in some way. For example, if you open your presentation with the question, "How can we retain our top talent in the current job market?" Your final statement might be, "Most importantly, top talent has to be identified early and continuously nurtured in order to be retained." This last thought loops back to your opening and provides closure to it.

RECAP:

  - Any public speaking situation creates an unspoken social contract where the audience agrees to devote its time and attention to the presenter, while the presenter is expected to deliver valuable and relevant information to them in return. We respect our part of this contract during the presentation by informing the audience how our message relates to or is beneficial to them.

  - Develop your presentation by following the five steps to a great business presentation structure.

  - In presenting and expanding on your main points, use details, examples, personal stories, expert sources, and data and statistics to provide support for your message.

  - Steps 2, 3, and 4 are essential, and are basically the structure, "Tell the audience what you are going to say, say it, then tell the audience what you've said," with the addition of the audience's needs and interests. But you can create a truly memorable presentation by also including Steps 1 and 5 in your structure, which provide an opening that grabs the listener's attention and finish with a takeaway statement.

RHETORICAL ASPECTS: TRANSITION WORDS, HUMOR, AND REPETITION

This chapter examines three types of common rhetorical devices you can use throughout your presentation to help reinforce your message and make your points sink in with the audience: transition words and phrases, humor, and repetition. Although all three have their place within a business presentation, the first is perhaps the most essential, while the extent to which you take advantage of the other two is more flexible.

Using transition words and phrases

Transition words and phrases are extremely useful in

structuring our thoughts so that the audience can follow a progression from one idea to another. They indicate to the audience when a particular idea has been fully expressed, when the next idea begins, and how they are connected to each other. As such, they form a critical part of a presentation that you should make sure to include.

You are already familiar with many types of transition words, as we use them in speech all the time to signal certain information to the listener. We call these words "signposts," because they typically appear at the beginning of a sentence and suggest what we're going to say next. You can emphasize these words and phrases by putting special intonation on them and pausing briefly after you say them.

Here are some signpost words that are commonly used in presentations, and what they usually indicate is coming next:

- However / In reality (introducing a contrast from what was just previously said)
- Moreover (reinforcing what was just now said)
- Actually (either contradicting another person's statement or expanding on our own thoughts)
- Likewise (comparing a new thought with one just expressed)
- Also (giving more information on a certain topic)
- In essence (extracting a key message from a larger point)
- Fortunately / Unfortunately (introducing pleasant / unpleasant news)
- Clearly / Obviously (stating a result from previously stated facts or opinions)
- Consequently (showing an effect of a situation or

action)
- Therefore (drawing a conclusion)

You can use these particular signposts, and others, to promote a smooth flow from one idea to another in a presentation.

Longer transition phrases also provide rhetorical structure and guide the audience through your presentation in a way that is easy for them to follow your flow of thoughts. Specific parts in your presentation will require these transition phrases to connect ideas together or to show a change. Below are some examples of some transition phrases and when in your presentation you would say them.

Introducing your presentation
- Today we're going to discuss/look at...
- This presentation will examine/focus on...
- As you already know, our topic today is about...

Outlining your presentation
- There are four major areas I'd like to cover in this presentation...
- This talk will consist of three sections...
- We'll first start with..., and after that take a look at...

Transitioning to your main topics
- Let's go to our first area of discussion, which is...
- I'd now like to start with my first point...
- Now that we've covered the basics of this talk, we can begin our discussion by looking at...

Highlighting a key point
- I want to emphasize how important this is...
- It is absolutely critical to understand that...

- A major concern of ours is that...

Referring back to a previous part of the presentation

- As you'll recall from earlier in the speech...
- I previously mentioned that...
- Going back for a moment to...

Bringing up a tangential comment

- And on that note, let me also say that...
- As an aside, I'd also like to point out that...
- Let me make an additional comment on that by saying...

Connecting a point with your overall message

- This provides us with further evidence that...
- This again shows that...
- We can see here how this relates to...

Transitioning to another point in your presentation

- Let's move on to the next point, which is...
- We can see another aspect of this through...
- Now that we've covered our first point, let's next examine...

Bringing up an example

- This point is best illustrated by...
- We can see how this works in practice by...
- Let's now take a look at a practical application of this...

Taking questions from the audience

- I'll be happy to take your questions now.
- Does anyone have any thoughts or questions on this?
- What do you all think about this?

Directing attention to your slides
- This next slide will clearly show that...
- The graph in this slide highlights that...
- I'd like to point out that in this diagram...

Summarizing your presentation
- Today we discussed three major points, the first being...
- I'd now like to go over once again...
- Let's review the key issues looked at in this presentation...

Concluding your presentation
- Let me leave you with the following thought...
- My final comment is...
- Above all, I want to emphasize that...

As with signposts, you should make these phrases stand out through a lively vocal delivery. But take care not to overuse any one signpost or transition phrase within a single presentation, as it will get repetitive. Employ a variety of them to keep your speech interesting. You could also complement some of these spoken phrases with pictures on your slides to provide your audience with a visual transition as well as a verbal one.

Using humor

The very thought of humor in a business presentation may come as a surprise to you. Is this the appropriate place for us to be funny? Doesn't it hurt our credibility if we come off as light-hearted? The specific answer really depends on each presentation, but what I don't want you to do is completely disregard humor as part of your rhetorical arsenal and assume that it is never appropriate at work.

Clearly, there are certain types of presentations in which it would not be appropriate to make jokes. These include when you have to communicate negative or critical information, or when you want to emphasize the gravity of your topic. In such cases, dropping humor into your presentation would undercut your message and likely confuse your audience. You may also prefer to hold back the jokes when you present in front of upper management, although ultimately this could depend on their individual personalities and how well you already know them.

But humor can be a powerful tool for presenters when appropriate to the topic and audience. One of the main benefits of humor is that it lightens the mood and makes everyone in the room feel relaxed and comfortable with you, creating an atmosphere receptive to your message. In addition, most people simply do not expect a business presentation to be funny at all, and it can be a pleasant surprise for many when it does appear.

Another positive effect of using humor is that it immediately engages the audience and creates a sense of bonding with them. It can also re-engage audience members who have been "tuning out" of your presentation. When these people hear others around them chuckling, they quickly snap back into attention, as humans are naturally curious about the interesting and fun thing that was just said.

Humor also makes your presentation memorable. You may have heard the axiom often given to public speakers, "People may not remember what you've said, but they'll remember how you've made them feel." This is absolutely true, and when you are able to make others laugh, or at least feel relaxed and comfortable during your talk, you impress a positive feeling in their minds that will remain with them long after your presentation is over.

For humor to work in a business presentation, it needs to be relevant to your message. This means that it should be connected to your topic in some way and make logical sense to say in the context of your speech. Ideally, it should also support your message by helping illustrate a main point or concept.

In my work as a corporate trainer, I often relate amusing stories to highlight a point in a way that will resonate with the audience better than a simple explanation. In one of them, I point out how we can still express ourselves successfully even if we can't always think of the exact words to say. I tell participants a story about a non-native English speaker who wanted to buy a chicken in a supermarket, but could not remember the word for it. This woman solved her language gap by picking up an egg and asking the employee nearest her, "Where's the mother?"

This joke only works because it connects to a larger point I am trying to make. If I told that story outside of that context, it would just appear to be a cheap attempt to make the audience laugh and get them to like me. So forget about telling any random jokes in your presentation simply because you think they are funny and want to loosen up your audience.

I've already mentioned my disapproval of opening a presentation with a joke. In addition to what I've already stated, starting a presentation with a joke doesn't really set the proper tone for a business presentation. Your intention may only be to lighten the mood from the start, but you also run the risk of appearing unprofessional. Begin your presentation on a serious note to show you should be taken seriously, and only use humor later at appropriate points.

Likewise, use humor selectively in your presentation, as it will work against you if you are always trying to be funny. Using too much humor in your talk will undercut your credibility and make it seem as if your message is not important enough to be taken seriously. So feel free to be funny in the right places, but don't overdo it.

A recent example from the news emphasizes how getting humor wrong in a presentation can have disastrous consequences, especially when it opens the talk and is not relevant to the topic. In July 2019, the chairman of the State Board of Elections in North Carolina, Robert Cordle, opened a meeting in front of hundreds of state election officials with a lengthy joke that compared cows to women as its punch line. Needless to say, Cordle's joke was completely unrelated to their jobs or to the reason why they were there.

Worse, one election official in attendance called it a "dirty joke" that was "misogynistic and wildly inappropriate for a high-ranking state official to tell." Unsurprisingly, enough audience members were so offended by Cordle's crude attempt at humor that he was forced to resign his position soon after this incident occurred.

Using repetition

Repeating information is an important way that people learn and remember new things, and you can make use of it to help your message sink in with the audience. I don't think enough presenters take advantage of the benefits of repetition to help them communicate their message.

The reason why repetition works as a rhetorical tool is

because the first time we hear someone say something it won't necessarily make an impact on its own. But when we hear it stated again, it is now something we are instantly familiar with and so lodges itself in our brain. This works whether it's a word or concept we already know or have just learned. Either way, hearing it repeated leaves an impression with the listener, causing us to involuntarily think to ourselves, "That must be really important if the presenter said it again."

We'll take a look here at two types of repetition used in business presentations, which I'll term "immediate repetition" and "motif repetition."

Immediate repetition: this is exactly what it sounds like – you say a word or phrase and then repeat it again before moving on. Doing this is useful when you want to either stress the importance of a particular term, or ensure that the audience has heard the phrase clearly.

To give an example, "This one change allowed our operating costs to decrease by 23% – 23% – in just one year." By repeating the percentage point, you draw the audience's attention to that number and elevate it in importance relative to other pieces of information. In most cases, you would also repeat this information differently the second time, saying it slower and louder, followed by a short pause to make sure it stands out.

But just as with humor, you should be selective when emphasizing information in this way. If you do it too often you will end up making too many things important, diluting the individual value of each item and making it hard for your audience to remember all of them. Your presentation style may also appear overly dramatic if you do this too much. Try not to use immediate repetition for emphasizing information more than 3-4 times within a single presentation.

Immediate repetition can also clarify a term or phrase that might not register with the audience the first time they hear it. Go through a draft of your presentation and make note of anything that your audience may not be familiar with or expect to hear in the context you plan to say it. These will usually be things like industry concepts, processes, acronyms, lesser-known businesses, government agencies, and other business jargon. All of them are potential candidates for immediate repetition, for example:

> *"We've decided to call this automated tool SRQ – S-R-Q – which stands for..."*

> *"This next slide shows how to display workflow on a kanban board – kanban board."*

When you repeat information for this purpose, you don't necessarily have to intonate the word or phrase any differently the second time. It's usually enough if you just slow down your rate of speech the second time to ensure the audience gets it. Repeating it in this way is like sending a message to the audience that says, "I just want to make sure you've heard this term correctly, as you may not be familiar with it or expect to hear it in this context."

Motif repetition: this involves repeating certain information throughout a presentation as a way of either making your audience remember a particular concept or framing your talk in a certain way. Repetition makes your idea or phrase more familiar with an audience, and people tend to remember things they are more familiar with. You want your audience to think, "I remember the presenter mentioning that earlier in the talk." This especially works best if they are able to connect your motifs with information they already know.

There are even examples of motif repetition in this book. In the next chapter, I'm going to introduce the concept of "presentational profile" and attempt to explain what I mean by it. But I want to make sure this concept sticks with you, so I also repeat it in later chapters both to identify new aspects of it as well as to remind you of the term itself. Using this same technique in your presentations ensures that your key concepts stick in the audience's mind.

You can also frame your talk in a certain way with motif repetition. Suppose you are giving a presentation on your company's charitable giving practices. You might claim at the start that the firm follows the "cycle of virtuous giving" (a term I have just made up for this example), and then explain what that means. Throughout the presentation, you could repeat the phrase again a few more times just to let the concept sink in with your listeners.

By the end, when you repeat the phrase "cycle of virtuous giving" in your conclusion for the last time, your audience will now know what you mean, or at least understand what you're referring to. You've also wrapped up the presentation in a satisfying way for the audience by looping back to your beginning.

But as with the other type of repetition, there is a limit to the benefits of this, and this technique loses its effectiveness if we repeat a phrase too many times. Your objective should be to repeat a phrase enough times so that it is memorable, but not so much that the audience starts to get sick of hearing you say it.

RECAP:

- Use signposts as transition words to show what kind of information you're going to say next. Use longer transition phrases at specific points in your presentation to help frame your speech and promote a smooth flow from one point to another.

- Use humor to engage your audience, and make it appropriate to the situation. But don't start your speech with a joke or overdo humor by trying to be funny too often.

- Use repetition to make your points stick with the audience. Immediate repetition makes an idea clear or memorable, especially if you say it in a different tone of voice. Motif repetition frames your message and makes your ideas more familiar to the audience. Use repetition selectively and don't use either form of repetition too often in any one presentation.

PREPARING TO DELIVER YOUR SPEECH

Up until now, we've mostly been concerned with how your speech looks on paper, meaning the content, structure, and rhetorical devices you actually speak in the presentation. We're now going to look at how your presentation appears and sounds to the audience, which is called *delivery*.

Presentation profile versus conversational profile

The first thing we should understand about delivery is that speaking in front of an audience requires a different set of behaviors from us than what we're normally used to. We can call this set of behaviors a *presentational profile*.

In contrast, a *conversational profile* is the regular set of behaviors that we display when we are in normal conversation with another person or a small group.

Our behavior in the conversational profile is quite familiar to us; these include aspects like maintaining eye contact only with our conversational partner, keeping the volume of our voice at a level so that only our partner can hear us and no one else, not moving around much or making large gestures while we speak, and so on. Taken together, these behaviors indicate to our communication partner that we are communicating only with them, and not with others outside of the conversation.

Our presentational profile, on the other hand, consists of a set of behaviors that we practice much less frequently than our conversational profile, and therefore does *not* come naturally to most of us. As a result, *presenters unfortunately often display their conversational profile when they speak in front of others, giving them a less-than-ideal presentational style.*

This shows up when presenters speak in a low voice, maintain limited eye contact with their audience, keep their movements small, and close their bodies off through their posture or specific gestures. As already noted, these behaviors are normal in one-to-one conversation, but generally unsuitable for presenting in front of a group of people.

We have to accept that delivering an effective presentation requires behaving in a way that is *not* our everyday manner of behavior. This is why it feels uncomfortable!

This doesn't mean you have to be a different person though. You can still be yourself, but the concept of different profiles allows us to present an alternate side of ourselves, one that helps us communicate our message more effectively. If you feel uncomfortable with practicing the specific delivery techniques suggested in the next few chapters, understand that it often takes time to get comfortable with your presentational profile.

Getting feedback from others

How do you know if your presentation delivery is effective? The truth is that we are not usually the best judges of our own delivery, as what feels most comfortable for us as a presenter is often not the best experience for the audience. This is why you should attempt to solicit feedback from a third party who can give you an objective, honest opinion of your performance.

Arrange someone to do this for you ahead of time. First identify someone who will be observing your presentation. This should be a person who can be honest with you, whose opinion you trust, and who is not your superior or one of the decision makers connected with your topic. If no one in your audience fits these criteria, you will have to wait for a future opportunity.

If you are able to find a suitable person, approach them and ask them to pay attention to how you deliver your presentation, noticing in particular how you speak and how you look during your talk. They should preferably take notes for you. Ask them to share these notes with you afterwards, and in return you can offer to evaluate their presentations in the future.

The next two chapters will cover specific ways you should look and sound as you deliver your presentation.

RECAP:

- Develop and adopt a "presentational profile," a set of behaviors that helps you transmit your message in the most effective way for the presentation format. This is distinct from your "conversational profile," which is more familiar to you. This means you will likely feel uncomfortable with your presentational profile at first, but you will eventually get used to it.

· Try to find someone before your presentation who will be in your audience, and ask them to evaluate your performance. Ask for specific feedback from them after the presentation. This should be someone you trust and who is not your superior.

VOCAL ELEMENTS OF YOUR DELIVERY

The vocal elements of your presentation, meaning how you sound while you present, are the most important part of your delivery. You have to ensure that they work effectively to deliver your message, because if your voice is used ineffectively, then your entire presentation will suffer. And for remote presentations, except for your slides, your voice may be the *only* tool you have to communicate your message. Let's look now at some ways that you can do this.

Volume – be heard!

It might seem obvious to some, but you have to be heard if you want to make sure your message gets through to the audience. This means speaking at a volume which the audience can hear you clearly.

When presenting in front of a small group, volume doesn't typically pose such a big problem to the presenter. In larger groups, it can be hard to make sure every word you say is clearly heard by everyone in the room without a microphone. In part, this is because human bodies absorb sound. The more people you have in your audience, the louder you will have to speak to make yourself heard.

Your voice should be loud enough that *100% of the audience can hear 100% of your presentation*. If only the first couple of rows can hear everything you say and those sitting behind them have to struggle to catch every word, your voice needs to be louder.

Unfortunately, our message can get completely lost even if the audience is able to hear, say, 80% of our presentation. This is because we don't focus on what we do hear, but rather on trying to fill in the missing words that we are unable to hear clearly. Our message struggles to get through as a result.

To fix this, first of all you need to recognize that your speaking voice should be louder than what you're typically used to. In other words, your presentational profile demands a louder speaking voice than your conversational profile, and you have to make a shift in your head to displaying your presentational profile.

Once you've made that shift, the next step is learning how to increase your volume without yelling. Yelling is not only undesirable because it is unpleasant to listen to, but also because it strains the vocal cords. Feel free in general to experiment with your voice while presenting, within limits, but avoid doing anything that puts strain and stress on your vocal cords.

How to do it: the solution to increasing your volume properly is to *project your voice*. This should be familiar to anyone who has had previous acting or vocal training, as it is a basic skill that actors and singers have to master. The way to do it is to breathe in a different way from the way you ordinarily breathe. In ordinary conversation, most people take shallow breaths that only partially fill up their lungs, and the air that is exhaled does not create a lot of sound.

But when you present, breathe deeply to let your lungs take in a large amount of air and expand to their fullest. As you exhale, your diaphragm, located directly below your lungs, raises and pushes out a large column of air. This allows you to forcefully project your voice and increase your speaking volume without it sounding unpleasant to the audience.

Projecting your voice is easier for some people than for others, but almost everyone is capable of projecting their voice into a room of up to 40-50 people with practice. Beyond a group of that size, you will most likely need a microphone and PA system. If you find that projecting your voice is a challenge for you, look up some breathing activities that you can practice to get better with this.

Energy – draw the audience to you!

One important component of voice that frequently gets overlooked is the energy we put into our voice. When your voice is full of energy, it keeps the audience's attention.

This is because displaying energy gets the audience's attention and creates interest. When people hear you speak excitedly about a topic, even something that they do not find inherently interesting, it stimulates their curiosity. At the very least, it makes them wonder why you are so interested in the topic. Conversely, a lack of energy in your voice communicates that you find your topic uninteresting, and you quickly lose their attention.

How to do it: make your voice enthusiastic and lively! For business presentations, enthusiasm for your topic is best expressed through the voice instead of the body. You appear professional when your voice displays energy but your body movements are restrained and under control.

This doesn't mean you have to show "passion." One piece of advice often given to public speakers is to "be passionate" about your topic, but I'm not convinced this is absolutely necessary for your business talks. You don't need to be passionate about a business-related topic like customer relationship management in order to give a great presentation about it, nor will it be expected from your audience either.

But putting at least some energy into your voice demonstrates to the audience the importance you attach to the topic. It also shows you care about making sure your message gets through.

Intonation – accentuate your speech!

You intonate speech when you change the way a given sound, word, or phrase is spoken. As listeners, we are all sensitive to changes in the voices we're listening to, whatever the context. Words that are intonated relative to other words around them get noticed.

Intonation is a vital way to communicate the relative importance of information in your presentation. Professionals have to deal with different kinds of information, but not all of it is equal in terms of importance. You indicate to the audience that certain information is more important by intonating those parts.

How to do it: there are basically three ways to change how you say a word: you can make it longer, louder, or in a different pitch. In practice, speakers typically use these in combination when they intonate, putting stress on a word by changing all three aspects at the same time.

Intonation not only gives extra importance to the words or sounds being said but also communicates underlying meaning. Think of saying the word "what" in a plain, neutral voice. Now think about saying "what" when someone has told you a piece of news that is unbelievable to you. You would say it quite differently in this case, raising your volume as well as your pitch, and also lengthening the vowel sound. These combined changes give additional information to the audience regarding not only the meaning of the word itself but also how we feel about it.

I recently asked a group of participants in one of my training courses to develop a short pitch for their department to a potential job applicant in just 45 seconds. When one person from the credit risk department of a bank gave her speech, three specific benefits of working in her department jumped out at me: you could "learn many things" about this area of banking, "do interesting work," and "work with a great team."

These particular phrases fixed themselves in my head because of how she said them. By intonating these parts of her speech, they functioned as "headings" within her speech that not only were memorable to the listeners but also provided her with sub-topics to expand upon further.

Speaking rate – get your timing right!

Pay close attention to the speed in which you speak during your presentation. You have to speak at the proper rate for your audience to be able to receive and process your message adequately.

An ideal speaking rate for presentations is around 125 words per minute. If you speak any slower than this, the audience will get bored and impatient as they wait for your words to come out.

But in general, speaking too fast tends to be more common than speaking too slow, so it is worth focusing more attention on this problem. When you speak at a rate faster than 150 words per minute, most people will find it difficult to follow your thoughts. As a result, your message, as well as individual details, gets lost on the audience.

It is also much harder to intonate your speech when you speak too fast. As explained in the previous section, intonating your speech allows you to emphasize certain information relative to other information and express how you feel about a certain topic, but fast speakers are unable to do this. You won't be able to highlight specific phrases in your speech and indicate which parts of it are more important than others.

How do you know if you are speaking at the proper rate? It can be tough to determine your accurate speaking rate in a real presentation. Before the talk, it's easy enough to figure out: simply count the number of words in your speech, then time yourself as you practice in front of a mirror or in an empty meeting room in your office.

However, the rate at which you speak while rehearsing on your own is almost certainly going to be different than when you give the presentation for real. In the latter case, your anxiety is usually heightened due to the pressure of the situation and as you become aware that all of the audience's attention is focused on you. This anxiety may be even greater if there are senior managers present or if your topic is critical for the company. In response, presenters often react to this feeling by unconsciously speeding up the presentation to "get it over with."

Another common mistake is when presenters gradually increase their speaking rate throughout their presentation. Their speed is fine at the start, but as it goes on, they lose focus and their anxiety has increased to the point where they've lost the ability to control it. They end up losing their audience along the way.

Another reason why presenters tend to speak too quickly is related to expertise. At work, we are often asked to give a presentation on a topic because we are qualified to speak about it. It may be because we have worked in this area extensively, or it is just related to what we do as part of our everyday job responsibilities.

This means you are presenting on a topic that may be well-known to you but not necessarily to those you are presenting to. Thus you tend to speak too quickly because of your familiarity with the topic. Even though you know your topic well, you have to remind yourself that your audience is hearing your words for the first time, and they need more time than you do to process your thoughts and connect them to the larger message.

How to do it: you need to remain conscious of how fast you are speaking throughout the entire presentation and adjust your speed accordingly by trying to stay at a rate of 125 words per minute. The problem with this is that you yourself are not always the best judge of whether you're speaking at the proper rate, because what feels right for you is often too fast for the audience.

If the rate in which you're speaking seems a bit too slow for you, it is possibly just right for the audience. And since presentations are for the benefit of your audience, you need to adjust to their needs instead of your own.

So get another opinion by asking for honest feedback about this from a neutral, third-party observer in the audience. Let that person know that you'd like them to pay attention to your speaking rate in addition to other parts of your delivery, then let you know what they think of it. You can use their feedback to adjust your speed in future presentations.

Pauses – let your thoughts sink in!

Taking pauses at the appropriate parts of your presentation lets you create dramatic tension, emphasize key parts of your message, and slow down your rate of speaking. You should take advantage of these benefits by putting a lot of pauses in your speech.

One communication trainer I've worked with refers to pauses as "punctuation for your speech," and it's a good comparison to use in understanding this area of speech delivery. Listening to presenters who don't take pauses while speaking is quite similar to reading a text without punctuation. Their message can be confusing and hard to figure out, and there doesn't seem to be much structure to the thoughts that build up the message. You get the feeling that the presenter is rushing through their thoughts and not emphasizing the importance of any information relative to anything else.

How to do it: punctuation marks that would appear in writing, especially the comma and period, are fairly good guides in helping us understand where to take a pause.

In general, we should take a short pause wherever there would be a written comma, and a longer pause wherever we might put a period.

Beyond this, taking pauses in other places will also improve your presentation delivery for two specific reasons, emphasis and dramatic effect.

Pause for emphasis: when you pause while speaking, the last thing you say before the pause will resonate a little longer inside the audience's head. This has the effect of emphasizing that idea or thought to the listener, so whenever you want to indicate that something is important and memorable, take a brief pause after you say it.

Certain proper names and data points are places in your speech that most likely deserve a pause. You should also pronounce these slightly slower than the rest of your speech. For names, think not only about names of people but also less familiar companies, departments, processes, tools, services, countries, and industries, or names of things that the audience does not expect to hear in the context you say them.

Let's say your team uses a software package named Alpha on a regular basis. Since your audience knows it well, you don't need to put a pause after it in your presentation. But when you mention how your team's efficiency will improve by switching to the Omega tool instead, taking a brief pause after the name lets the less familiar word sink in and resonate with the audience for a moment.

You can also do this for data points. Percentages, fractions, monetary amounts, and other quantities are key content information for business presentations. It is critical that these be clearly heard, and that your listeners have time to absorb their importance, especially when you are making comparisons. If your presentation contains a large number of data points, they will not all be of equal importance. Decide which ones are most critical for your audience to reflect on and take a pause after saying them.

For acronyms, you should not only slow down your speech as you pronounce each letter and pause briefly at the end, but also state what the acronym stands for if you think your audience might not know it. Here's an example: "Many of you have heard about the CCA – *Comprehensive Credit Analysis* – Project and how it will be the main focus of our team for the next quarter. This talk will be a formal overview that project."

Pause for dramatic effect: you generate added interest in your topic by also taking a pause *before* you state important information. Just don't overdo this in any given talk, as business presentations are not the proper venue to present information in an overly-dramatic manner. But doing this selectively in your presentation is acceptable, particularly if it refers to information that reflects positively on you or your team.

Pitch – get the tone right!

Pitch is the musical tone of a sound. Each of our voices has a natural pitch range, the range of tones that we naturally speak in without having to strain our voices. In much the same way, singers perform in specific ranges that are natural for them. We adjust the pitch of our voices when we say something in a higher or lower tone.

There is no "right" pitch for you to speak in, as it is different for each person. But in general, presentations delivered in a lower pitch tend to sound richer and more pleasing to the audience than in a higher pitch. Business presentations given in a lower pitch also impart authority and make you appear more serious and credible to the audience.

How to do it: speak at a slightly lower pitch while presenting than you might in normal conversation with another person, but still within your natural pitch range. This is another aspect of your "presentational profile."

Just make sure that the pitch you speak in does not strain your vocal cords, which are located in your larynx or voice box. You should avoid any low or high tones that put a strain on your vocal cords, as this strain is an indication that you are speaking outside of your natural pitch range.

I recommend recording your presentations if you have the opportunity to do so, and paying attention to this lesser-regarded aspect of vocal quality.

Articulation – be clear with your words!

When you articulate, you enunciate speech so that the sounds come out clear and distinct and the audience does not have to struggle to understand what you say. You don't slur words or have sounds run together in an unintelligible way.

How to do it: clearly enunciate every sound that comes out of your mouth. Good vocal quality for presentations requires that you pay close attention to articulation.

This is a foundational aspect of vocal quality similar to volume, in that if you do not articulate your speech, then the audience has to shift its focus to trying to understand the words you're saying instead of the message you're trying to convey. Using your voice in other ways, such as intonating words and pausing, becomes pointless when the audience struggles to comprehend your speech.

But be mindful to not overdo your articulation either. Your goal should be to ensure that the sounds you make are clear and comprehensible, but not overdone. When you overarticulate speech, you pronounce words individually and not link them together in a way that sounds natural, resulting in speech that sounds artificial and robotic. Obviously, this is not a desirable quality for your voice.

In your presentational profile, you should take greater care in articulating words than when in casual conversation with others. You can be more lax with speech in conversations because your partner can simply ask you to repeat any words or phrases that weren't clear to them. In the middle of a presentation, however, members of the audience are less likely to speak up when they don't understand. Make it easy for the audience to stay focused on your message by articulating a little clearer than is otherwise normal for you.

Vocal changes – shake things up!

The advice given thus far in this chapter showed you the best general ways to use your voice when giving a presentation. Following it consistently will undoubtedly give you a strong vocal quality when you present, which may be enough for novice presenters.

But you can take your delivery to a higher level by adding *vocal changes* to the mix. The idea behind this is that at certain points in your talk you can enhance your delivery by deviating from the standard practice. Suddenly slowing down your rate, or speaking briefly in a louder or lower voice, for example, adds something extra to your vocal delivery.

Changing your voice keeps the audience engaged in your topic and pulls them back in if their attention has been drifting away. This is simply because people notice changes, but "zone out" when things stay the same. In the case of vocal delivery, a voice that doesn't change becomes uninteresting to the audience after a period of time, even if it otherwise has great vocal quality. By making a change every now and then in the appropriate place, you generate immediate interest.

This concept is not new to you if you've ever enjoyed listening to someone tell a good story. Compelling storytellers engage us precisely because they change their voices in a way that enhances the story and brings it alive. Presenting on a topic at work is not exactly the same thing as storytelling, but we can use similar techniques to keep an audience hooked on our speech.

How to do it: vocal changes are most effective when you primarily change four elements of your speech: volume, energy, pitch, and rate. Intonation and speech pauses are different since they are already a type of vocal change, and you probably shouldn't change your articulation much for business presentations, as making your speech any less distinct is not likely to provide you any benefits. But you can definitely alter your voice in the other four ways mentioned here.

And just like intonating words a certain way, changing your voice at certain points also makes those parts more memorable to the audience. Suppose there's a line in your presentation like, "These results appear to show that our latest ad campaign has been a complete success." You could make this key statement stick in your audience's head by, for example, slowing down this sentence, saying it with higher energy and conviction, and perhaps even in a noticeably lower pitch than the rest of your presentation.

The key to using vocal changes properly is making sure they match the content you are saying. If you have your presentation written down, you can usually locate places in the text that lend themselves to certain changes. Print it out and make written notes at the parts you think would be enhanced by altering your voice. These could be where you are making contrasts, stating extremes, quoting another person, or words that carry strong emotional resonance, such as "huge" or "unprecedented."

Not matching your vocal changes to your content can lead to strange and less than favorable results. I was once at a conference watching a presenter with an odd and unpleasant style of delivery, but at first I wasn't certain was the problem was. She was putting a lot of vocal changes in her speech – sometimes speaking faster than normal, slowing down at a certain point, speaking in a high pitch, or making her voice excited and energetic.

The problem, which I eventually recognized, was that the changes she was making to her voice weren't actually connected to what she was saying, but appeared to be done more or less randomly. These changes felt artificially created just to keep the audience engaged and make them pay attention to her, resulting in a very ineffective delivery style. To make sense to the audience, the vocal changes you make have to derive naturally from the words you say.

Since vocal changes tend to give dramatic flair to your style, you shouldn't use them too often. Being professional means, in part, that you maintain a moderated tone and don't let your presentation style overpower your message. On the other hand, if you rarely or never make changes to your voice, you lose an excellent opportunity to enhance your message and make a strong impression with the audience.

RECAP:

- Speak at a volume that everyone in the audience can hear everything you say
- Put energy in your voice to draw the audience into your speech
- Intonate specific words and phrases to give emphasis to them and provide underlying meaning
- Speak at a rate at which everyone can understand you – around 125 words per minute is best
- Take pauses at appropriate places in your speech for emphasis and occasionally for dramatic effect
- Adjust your pitch so that you speak in a low, rich tone of voice
- Articulate your voice so that every sound that comes out of your mouth is clear and distinct
- Make vocal changes at appropriate points throughout your presentation to keep the audience engaged and interested in your speaking voice. These will mostly be changes in your volume, energy, pitch, and rate of speaking.

VISUAL ELEMENTS OF YOUR DELIVERY

Now that we've seen how to use our voice, let's explore how we should look, stand, and move when we're presenting in front of others. There are five basic elements of our visual presence that create a strong presentational delivery: eyes, stance, body movement, posture, and hand movement.

Eyes – form a bond with the audience

People are usually aware of the importance of making eye contact with the audience while presenting, at least in theory. But this is a lot trickier than they realize, and it's an area that most of us could improve upon.

Apart from the voice, your eyes are the part of the body that most engages the audience and draws them into your message. When you lock eyes with individuals watching your presentation, you give them the feeling that you are talking directly to them and personalizing your presentation to them in a visual sense.

Where you look can also direct the audience's attention, especially if you coordinate it with gestures. If you look at the slides, at something you're holding, or to your side, the audience's focus will also be directed at those places.

Presenters send messages with where they place their gaze. Darting your eyes around the crowd transmits that you are nervous and anxious, and perhaps lack the confidence or self-assurance to look any one person directly "in the eye."

Breaking eye contact also sends a message to the audience that is not preferable. When presenters break eye contact they most commonly look upwards or downwards.

If you look up during your presentation, you are usually communicating that you don't know what to say next. But if this is the case, you don't need to indicate that you are searching for the right words or are uncertain of what to say next, and in fact you shouldn't do this.

Likewise, you don't want to break eye contact by looking down either. Looking down, like looking up, also gives the impression that you are unsure of what to say next, but with the additional disadvantage of body language that projects a lack of confidence as well.

Don't give any visual indication that you don't know what to say next. A few years ago, I asked a question of a US ambassador after she had given a speech at the company I was working at overseas. She first seemed to fumble with her answer, but I was impressed that she remained confident and never broke eye contact with me. After about half a minute or so she managed to provide me with a suitable answer, but because she maintained strong eye contact with me the entire time, I'm sure that most of the others in attendance didn't even realize that she had initially stumbled.

How to do it: your eyes should remain on the audience whenever you don't have to avert your gaze somewhere else, like to your notes. Your goal is to make a connection with every person in our audience through eye contact. You don't make a connection when you scan the audience randomly, or dart your eyes from person to person. Nor do you connect with everyone when you only lock eyes with a selected number of audience members and ignore the others.

Making a connection through eye contact requires forming a *visual bond* with individuals while speaking. Focus your gaze on a particular person as you develop a thought or idea, then make eye contact with someone else as you transition to a different thought or idea. You can also combine a change in eye contact to a different audience member with changes in body movement, gestures, and vocal changes at the same time.

Forming a visual bond through eye contact is relatively easy when there are only a small number of people watching your presentation, as there are a limited number of eyes to focus on. But what about when there are not eight people in the audience, but 18? Or 80? Or much larger? How do you handle eye contact with so many people, and is it even possible?

Admittedly, making eye contact with individual audience members becomes more of a challenge the larger they are. For larger audiences, make eye contact with them in small groups by focusing on one person in that group. Eventually you will reach the entire audience and cover every "group" through the effective use of eye contact.

When presenting to a sizeable group of people, avoid making eye contact only with a limited number of people in the audience. It can be intimidating to stand up and see a huge audience focus its attention on you at one time, but resist the temptation to deal with it by only looking at the 10 or so people sitting in the front row and ignoring everyone else. Also resist only looking at people you know, or just those who look friendly.

And don't forget about people who may be sitting off to your sides. Take note of where your entire audience is located and make sure to include everyone who is watching you, no matter where they're seated. You don't need to make eye contact with people who are involved in the program, such as the person who introduced you, unless they sit down in the audience area.

It may not be an exaggeration to say that how you use your eyes while presenting can make or break your presentation. Anyone you do not make eye contact with will feel excluded, and is unlikely to be receptive to your message. But those you do create a visual bond with will form a connection to you as a presenter and will be more accepting of what you have to say.

Stance – be well-grounded

The next area of visual presence is how to stand when you give your presentation. You might sometimes sit down for smaller, less formal situations, but standing while you present tends to put you into your presentation profile and encourage a mindset conducive to proper style. This also applies when you give presentations remotely.

How to do it: when you stand while presenting, keep your legs about shoulder width apart, although women often prefer to keep their legs closer than shoulder width. Your feet should be slightly turned outward, either parallel to each other or with one foot slightly in front of the other, and firmly planted on the floor.

Your legs should not be stiff and rigid, but relaxed. Keep your weight evenly balanced on each leg as you present. When you move from one place to another, you should end up in this preferred stance when you stop.

Even though it sounds simple and straightforward, in practice many people find it a challenge to stand this way throughout their presentation. The biggest mistakes I see are crossing one leg in front of another, leaning on one leg, and uncontrolled movement in the legs or hips. Let's take a brief look at each of these.

Crossing legs: when you cross one leg in front of (or sometimes behind) another, you typically have to put nearly all of your body weight on the uncrossed leg. Your body then becomes less stable, as your crossed leg may not be able to balance your body adequately. And when you become unstable, you may have to hold onto something like a chair, wall, or table to steady yourself.

By doing this, you create an image in the audience's mind that is unflattering to your credibility. If you have to steady your physical body, it creates the impression that your message is also unsteady and not firmly grounded either.

Worse, the uncrossed leg tends to tire after a period of time, as it is bearing your full body weight. You will then have to shift your weight from one leg to another by uncrossing and crossing the other leg. Before long, the movements of crossing and uncrossing your legs will be distracting to the audience.

Leaning on one leg: even more common is when presenters lean onto one leg. When you do this, your body typically slumps over to the side as you put most of your body weight on that leg and your entire posture is awkwardly tilted off-balance. This is again not a posture that enhances credibility.

It is possible to maintain an upright posture with this kind of stance, but after a while many people shift their weight to their other leg and lean on that one, then later shift back to the first leg. You end up swaying back and forth as you unnecessarily move your body weight from leg to the other.

Uncontrolled leg movement: this occurs when you do not have a firmly-planted stance. It can include moving your leg forward and back, rocking side to side at the hip, and flexing your knee by lifting your heel up and down. Even if the uncontrolled movement is not rapid and does not give the impression of nervous energy, it does not inspire confidence in the audience that you are sure of your message and your ability to communicate it.

Oddly, presenters who have these kinds of problems with their stance generally lack awareness of what is happening beneath their waists. I have coached clients who appear to have a strong awareness and control of body movements above the waist, such as gestures, head movements and eye contact, yet their body parts below the waist seem to move on their own. Focused as they are on other aspects of the presentation, they are simply not paying attention to this area of their body and whatever's happening there.

When I coach individual clients with this problem, I ask them to deliver their presentation to me while not moving anything below their waist. They have to speak with upper body movement only, and later we reintroduce movement to their lower bodies. We then practice lower-body movement that is conscious and directed. If you don't have a speech coach to help you with this, you can try doing it yourself in front of a full-length mirror where you can see your whole body when you practice your presentation.

Body movement – be directed as you move around

Body movement refers to how we move around in our presentation space. Presenters do not often know how they should move around, but usually just do what "feels right" in the moment. But there are important things to keep in mind regarding this aspect of delivery.

First of all, you probably do not need to move your body around as much as you think you do. Most of the time you can give a perfectly decent business presentation of five minutes or less with very little body movement at all by simply standing in place as you speak and gesture. Any presentation longer than that probably would benefit from some stage movement, although this is not a strict rule, and it depends on the subject of your talk and your personal style. But even then, presenters tend to move around more than is probably necessary.

One notable exception to this is a presentation intended to motivate or inspire the audience, which tends to include a lot of movement. Those who have seen videos of speeches by former Microsoft CEO Steve Ballmer in his particularly animated style recognize how his energetic movement around the stage is designed to fire up and energize his employees.

How to do it: if you move in your presentational space, it should appear directed and intentional, and not as if you were just wandering around randomly. Don't feel you need to walk around a lot just because you have a large space to present in and want to cover as much of it as you can. Doing this looks like random movement, as it does when presenters pace back and forth on stage.

Once you've started moving, walk in a slow and steady manner to a specific location in your presentation area. When you've reached your desired location, stop and ground yourself with the type of stance discussed in the previous section. Make it appear as if you knew exactly where you were going, and that you intended to come to the exact spot where you've ended up.

It is also a good idea to integrate body movement with other aspects of delivery, like eye contact and gestures. When you transition to a new idea or concept in your speech, you can mark this change by simultaneously moving your eyes to another person in the audience, gesturing, and consciously moving towards the part of the audience you are making eye contact with. You can also accentuate this change even more by making vocal changes at the same time.

When you open a presentation, step forward towards the audience as you begin speaking. Doing this is usually perceived by the audience as a sign of confidence from the presenter, and it draws attention to you from the start. A step towards the audience combined with a memorable opening line delivered in a confident tone of voice will generate interest in your presentation right from the beginning, and it goes a long way towards keeping the audience's interest throughout.

You should also be conscious of the location where you begin your presentation. Wherever you start, face the audience and imagine that there's an imaginary wall behind you. You can move forward and back in your space, but not further back than from where you started, where you imagine your "wall" is. There are two reasons why you should do this.

The first reason is to avoid stepping backwards when you begin your presentation. This is a common error that can happen with less experienced presenters, especially in front of larger groups of people. When they turn to face the audience, these presenters get overwhelmed by the visual attention being showered on them, and inadvertently take a step backwards before they start to speak.

This is a highly undesirable way to start your presentation. Since stepping forwards when you start a presentation is generally interpreted by the audience as a sign of confidence, stepping backwards gives an indication that you lack confidence. The audience may even feel that you lack the knowledge needed to speak credibly on this topic.

In addition, picturing an imaginary wall behind where you start can help you avoid the phenomenon of "backwards creep." This occurs when you have a strong start to your presentation, but as it progresses, you struggle to cope with the attention and pressure, and gradually move towards the back of their presentation area. Presenters will even sometimes practically hide themselves behind a flipchart or lectern on stage.

When this happens, the presenter is trying to decrease the attention on themselves, even if they're not conscious of it. At the same time, they direct the audience's attention to their slides and effectively become just a narrator to their slide deck, virtually unseen.

Be aware of your body movement and how it will be perceived by the audience. When you do move around, make sure it is directed and intentional instead of random and unfocused.

Posture – stand tall and confident

The way you stand tells people a lot about you. Others can tell if you are confident and determined, or insecure and lacking confidence, just based on your posture. This is true in any situation, but it's especially critical when a group of people is focusing its attention on you and how you look.

Most of the time the posture that you have off the presentation stage is the same one you carry onto the stage. This means adopting good posture habits in everyday life makes it easier to maintain the proper posture for a business presentation. It also contributes to the impression your coworkers and teammates have of you at work, including when you present to them.

You should avoid a posture where your head is held far in front of your chest, so that the top of the spine is not in alignment with the rest of the spine below it. This inevitably leads to you lowering your head, having a hunched-over back, and your shoulders rotated forward.

When you adopt this posture, it also sinks the chest inward, giving you a defensive appearance. And since your head is lowered you are not able to make yourself as tall as you are physically capable of being. The result is a posture that doesn't enhance your authority on the topic or convince the audience to believe in you.

Another undesirable posture type is what I call the

"slacker" posture. This is when presenters push their hips and abdomen forward and lean their torso back, oftentimes leaning slightly to the side as well. Occasionally my coaching clients will say that they like this kind of posture, as it projects an attitude of casualness that some find appealing. It puts them at ease to see a person looking so relaxed while delivering a presentation.

This kind of posture may work at certain companies with more of an easy-going atmosphere, such as startups with younger workers. But it is so relaxed that I don't believe it commands respect from the audience or inspires confidence that you are a knowledgeable and credible speaker on your topic. Unless you are the CEO or owner of the company, in which your credibility derives largely from your position, I recommend that you avoid adopting the "slacker" posture.

How to do it: imagine that there is a length of string going through the middle of your body and coming up through the top of your head. Now envision that someone is pulling on the string and making it completely taut. This will lift your head straight up and make it align with your back, lifting your chin up as well and making you as tall as you are physically able to be.

It will also raise your chest slightly, puffing it out and keeping your back straight. When you adopt this posture you prominently display your upper body to the audience, indicating that you believe in your message and your communication skills.

As you stand in this posture, also make an effort to rotate your shoulders slightly further back than normal and hold them there. This again makes your chest prominent, showing your willingness to display your upper body and thereby projecting greater confidence to the audience.

But don't hold your shoulders back too far, as the resulting body posture will make you look overly-confident and arrogant.

The audience will notice these non-verbal signals about you even before you begin to speak, so ensure that your posture is in the right position as soon as their attention is turned toward you. As with any first impression, it can be harder to change others' opinion of you if you don't start off properly.

Hand movements – make your gestures support your message

Hands pose one of the biggest dilemmas for presenters. What do we do with them? Hold them stiffly next our sides? Behind us? In front? Move them around? Grab the lectern? All of the above?

I suspect that many people would prefer that their hands simply vanished when they get up to present. They could then avoid having to deal with yet another thing to think about during the presentation. This may be why presenters often hold their arms and hands in ways that are not conducive to a good presentational style.

Let's first take a look at some of the problematic ways of holding our arms and hands, then discuss how to use them effectively.

The "strong leader" position: this is when one hand clasps the wrist of the other arm behind your back. This puffs your chest out and tends to encourage a stiff, upright upper body posture, although you could also be stooped over when you have your arms in this position too. This arm posture does in fact "solve" the dilemma of what to do with your arms – just putting them behind you so they are no longer something you have to think about, but otherwise I don't recommend it.

Keeping your hands behind your back like this creates the image of a dominating authority figure, as if you were a prison warden, drill sergeant, or perhaps a wise college professor, depending on how else you look and act while in this pose. The audience may perceive you as strong and confident, but you are also likely to seem intimidating or coldly distant to them. Even if this is the image you *want* to project of yourself, you won't likely be warmly received by the audience. And projecting this image would be quite inappropriate for employees who are not in a leadership position in the company.

Beyond the image you project, there are two other problems with this arm posture. First, holding your arms behind your back does not invite the audience into your speech, preventing you from connecting with them. Second, you also eliminate the possibility of allowing your arms and hands to support your message, which is a lost opportunity for you to communicate your message better.

There is one case though in which the "strong leader" pose might be advisable: when you are afflicted with uncontrollably shaky hands. If you are truly unable to stop your hands from shaking due to nervousness, it may be best to just hold them behind your back so that the shaking doesn't distract from your message.

Crossing your arms: having your arms crossed in front of you while presenting is generally comfortable for most people, and it again provides a solution for those who don't know what to do with their hands. But despite the temptation, it's generally not good to cross your arms in front of you for the same reasons as why you shouldn't hold them behind you: you eliminate the possibility of arm and hand movement, preventing you from making a stronger connection with the audience and using them to support your message.

But it's even worse than the "strong leader," as covering your torso makes you appear closed off to the audience. In fact, anything blocking the audience from seeing your torso for a long period of time will make you appear this way.

How to do it: move your hands and arms so that they support your words. The specific way to do this will vary from person to person, depending on personality, the nature of the topic, and individual presentation style, but there are a few common elements that work for most everyone.

When making gestures, think of your upper limbs as a physical way to express your message, or an extension of the words you are saying at the moment. You can use your whole body to do this too to some extent, but your hands are more of a focal point for the audience.

Always make sure your hands and arms are visible to the audience if possible. This can mean merely holding them loosely to your side while you present if you wish. But don't hide your hands or arms in any way, such as putting them in your pants pockets.

It also means getting out from behind a lectern to openly face the audience, unless your microphone is attached to it. A lectern can obscure your gestures and hide your hands, as well as your entire lower body. You will appear more open and confident if the entire front of your body is visible to the audience and not hidden behind a lectern.

If you have a lectern, I recommend using it only to hold any notes or index cards you may need. If you have to refer to your notes, you can go over to the lectern and briefly look at them, but otherwise try not to stand behind it for long periods of time.

In general, you should keep your hands apart from one another as much as possible. You can bring them together occasionally, but only when doing so supports your message. The problem is that holding your hands together creates a physical block between your torso and the audience, and it also limits your ability to use your hands for expression. Instead, keeping your hands mostly apart opens up your midsection and demonstrates to the audience that you are credible, trustworthy, and confident.

When your hands are together there is an opportunity for them to engage in unconscious, undesirable movement. These include pulling on your fingers, twisting rings, squeezing one of your hands, or playing with your watch. Since your audience's attention will be drawn to whatever hand movement you make, these movements take attention away from where you want it to be focused.

For similar reasons, try to avoid holding anything in front of you for too long while you present. These may be agendas, books, a product prototype, or any other object you can pick up. As with holding your hands together, there can be a temptation to unconsciously toy with these objects while you speak, creating more visual distractions for the audience.

It sometimes seems like presenters hold on to objects like books or sheets of paper with both hands as a kind of psychological shield to protect them against the overpowering weight of the attention from the audience. But avoid the temptation to do this, and only hold an object with one hand if at all possible, then put it down on a table or lectern when it isn't needed.

While you obviously need your slide advancing tool as you present, put that down as well when you don't need it. When you do need to use it, try to hold it so that you can still gesture while you have it in your hand.

Beyond this advice, the extent to which you use your hands to gesture is largely up to you and your personal style. Many people feel comfortable restricting their hand and arm movements by just occasionally making small movements with their lower arms and hands. This is fine if it works for you and your style.

But when you start to feel more comfortable in front of an audience, you can express yourself better by raising your arms and making broader gestures as you speak. You'll be better able to transition into this broader style of gesturing by imaging it as part of your presentational profile.

You can also put more energy in your arms and hands when making large, prominent gestures. For example, you can show you feel strongly about something by tensing up your arms, making a fist, and bringing down your hand in a forceful manner. Or you may wish to spread your arms apart, opening your palms and separating your fingers to indicate surprise or accentuate a certain point.

Your gestures make key information in your speech memorable in much the same way that changing your voice does, especially when the movements are broader and energetic. In most cases you shouldn't have to think too hard about what exact kind of gesture you should make, but just let your arms react in a natural way that accurately reflects what you are already expressing in your speech and tone of voice.

Unless you are using your gestures to make a forceful point, focus on keeping your arms and hands relaxed and not tense as you present. Sharp arm and hand movements indicate urgency and tension to the audience, while slower, more flowing movements show you are confident and in control. Extending your fingers outward to make your palm flat also indicates tension, as you have to tense up the muscles in your lower arms to do this.

Conversely, you look natural and at ease when your palms are held slightly cupped and fingers slightly curved. Displaying your palms to the audience by holding them upward or to the side makes you appear open and non-threatening.

But when you hold your hands outward with your palms facing down, you display authority and give off a commanding air. Moving your hands in an up and down motion when your palms face downward demonstrates an attempt to control a situation or other people.

Large gestures can be useful in helping you draw attention to certain points, but don't be too excessive with them. Unless you have a naturally oversized personality, putting a lot of big gestures into a single presentation will make you appear overly dramatic and decrease the perception of your professionalism. Another problem with overdoing large gestures is that it can be hard for the audience to distinguish key points from lesser ones – nothing receives any particular emphasis when you use broad gestures to accentuate everything.

Whatever gesture you make and however you decide to hold your hands, be sure it reflects what you really want to communicate to your audience.

RECAP:

- Keep your eyes focused on the audience as much as

possible, and try to form a "visual bond" with individuals, only breaking away when you start a new thought. Make sure you cover the entire audience through eye contact, not leaving out people sitting on your sides.

- Adopt a stance where your feet are well-grounded, about shoulder-width apart, and your body weight is balanced on both legs. Keep your legs relaxed and not stiff and rigid. Avoid any uncontrollable leg or hip movement that will be distracting to the audience.

- Make your movement in your presentation space directed and intentional, so that it doesn't look like random wandering. Be aware that you may not need to move around as much as you think you do, and after you move, stand in place and adopt the preferred stance above.

- Demonstrate a confident and commanding posture by imagining that a string is coming out through the top of your head and is pulling your body straight upwards. Hold your shoulders slightly back and keep your chin up as you present.

- Move your hands and arms so that they act as a natural extension of your words. Keep them visible to your audience and mostly apart from one another. Hold any objects with one hand only, if possible, and put them down on a surface when not needed. Let your gestures also be a natural reflection of your personality and individual style.

OTHER ASPECTS: TAKING QUESTIONS, USING SLIDES, REMOTE PRESENTING

This section will focus on three essential areas of the presentation experience: taking questions from the audience, creating and displaying slides, and presenting remotely, meaning presentations to an audience not in the same room as you.

Taking questions

Most business presentations include a period of time when the presenter takes questions from the audience. I've even heard of presentations where the presenter only has a minute to describe a single slide on a project they're working on, then has to spend the rest of the presentation time answering questions. In this case, the Q&A session *is* the presentation, or at least the most important part of it.

Taking questions from your audience is an excellent way to engage your audience directly and personalize your presentation. You can also use this time to demonstrate your competence on a topic and enhance your credibility, so make sure you allow ample time for Q&A and not shy away from it when you present.

There are two standard ways of taking questions during a presentation: either taking questions during your talk or after you've covered your material. Whichever you choose, make your preference clear to the audience near the beginning of your presentation.

You can be direct about this with statements like,

"I'll be happy to take your questions as we go through, so feel free to interrupt me at any time if something isn't clear."

"Please hold your questions until the end, when we'll have plenty of time to address your concerns."

If you have someone introducing you before you present, you could also ask that person to state your preferred way to take questions during their introductory remarks.

When an audience member asks you a question, immediately engage with that person through eye contact. This is not the best time to reach down and take a drink of water or let your eyes wander around the room, especially if the person asking is a manager or your boss.

For presentations in front of a large number of people, the audience may have access to a microphone to ask their questions. If there is no microphone for the person asking a question and there are people seated behind them, always make sure to repeat the question so that everyone in the audience has heard it. Not repeating the question in this kind of situation can be frustrating for the audience if not everyone heard what was asked. It also gives you, as the presenter, the chance to restate a confusing or complicated question in your own words and make it easier for you to answer it.

Following this, involve the entire audience in your answer, no matter how relevant you think the question is to everyone. Don't focus your attention solely on the person asking the question, but bring the audience into the exchange through the normal way of making eye contact and forming visual bonds with every person as you give your answer.

In other words, your Q&A is not a series of one-on-one talks with individual audience members, and it should not be thought of that way. Remember that the entire audience is still devoting its time and attention to your presentation during the Q&A session, and you respect that by showing that you want to include them in this discussion.

And don't assume that a highly specific question from one person doesn't have any relevance to the others present and that they won't be interested in it. It may be more widely applicable than you think. That said, try to make a specific question more relevant to a wider range of situations by connecting how it could apply in a more general sense to others.

Think of the person who asked the question as your visual "anchor," and check back with them occasionally through eye contact. Observe their facial and body language to ensure that they are following along with you and appear satisfied with your answer. If you see them giving any signs of visible disagreement with you such as shaking their head or frowning, modify your response or ask them a question to clarify matters for you.

Business presenters commonly respond to a comment with a statement like, "Why don't we discuss this together after the presentation?" or "I think we should take this matter offline." The idea behind this is not to waste the larger audience's time when you are absolutely certain that the question is only particular to you and the person asking it.

While saying this shows that you are thinking of the broader audience's needs, you can make yourself appear more competent and knowledgeable by first giving a brief answer to the question before suggesting to discuss it later in private. This tells the audience that you have an answer to the question and are not merely trying to dismiss it out of hand.

But what about when you really don't know the answer to a question? It is perfectly legitimate to acknowledge this when it happens, as long as you don't do it too frequently. You'll still appear competent if you respond in a strong and confident voice with a statement like:

This is a good question, and one in which we still need to find an answer to.

I'm glad you asked about this. We'll have to look again at the data and let you know.

Even so, you should make an effort before the presentation to anticipate what kind of questions you might be asked and how you would respond to them. Few things will kill your professional credibility faster than declaring ignorance on every question about your topic. Pay particular attention to unpleasant topics, like weak sales, decreasing market share, missed deadlines or targets, and so forth. If you choose not to address these areas in your presentation, anticipate being asked about them in the Q&A.

When finishing up a longer response to a question, turn back to the person who asked it and make eye contact with them again as you conclude, ensuring that they appear satisfied with your answer. Offer a brief smile while maintaining eye contact to indicate your gratitude for the question, and perhaps thank them verbally as well. With this you indicate that your answer is complete and that you are now open to receiving questions from others.

Making and using slides

Slides are one of the most enduring and ubiquitous aspects of business presentations. Although there are certainly business presentations that don't have a slideshow, your slides impart a sense of professionalism to your speech that it doesn't have without them, as well as a tool that helps you express your message.

Slides provide two basic benefits to the presenter: complementing your key points and helping the audience understand complex material. Let's examine each of these in detail.

Complementing key points: slides serve to reinforce your spoken words through pictures, quotes, or examples that are best communicated visually. They should not be used to make your points by themselves, so that you don't even need to give the presentation.

Occasionally my workshop participants tell me that they don't pay much attention to a presenter when they can just get the necessary information from that person's slides. This tells me that the presenter is *not* using slides to reinforce their message, but rather is *primarily* delivering most of their information this way. If so, then what is the point of giving a presentation at all? The presenter might as well just send everyone the slideshow by email and skip the presenting part altogether if they're not even needed.

We need to make our slides serve us, not the other way around. One communication professional, Zoltán "Dr. Prezi" Németh, puts it this way, "At least 80% of the audience's focus should be on the presenter, while no more than 20% of their focus should be on the slides." Your slides should be designed so that they keep the audience engaged and interested in your speech, but not to the extent that they overshadow you as the presenter.

Sometimes all you need is the right image to make your point stick. In one of my training sessions, I state that we are always communicating non-verbally around us. I then show the participants a picture of a group of people in an office meeting looking bored and detached while a man is speaking, and ask the group, "What are the people in the meeting communicating to the speaker?" My point about non-verbal communication in meetings is made immediately clear and memorable to the audience.

Help the audience understand and remember complex material: business presentations may contain a large amount of data or other complex information that can be dry or difficult to communicate through spoken language only. Displaying this information graphically on a slide in a graph, chart, or picture is typically the most common and effective way to present it in your presentation.

When you display data or other complex information on the slide, frame it in a specific way that makes your point for you. Each slide should have a single point to impress upon the audience. You can state this point explicitly through slide titles, and present the data in a way that supports the point you're making.

A neutral slide title would be "Call center average handling time." Instead of this, you could title your slide, "Overall improvement in average handling times" to highlight the specific improvement areas you want the data to emphasize. Ask yourself how the data can serve you, and adjust the information on your slide accordingly.

Creating your slides

When you design your slides, adopting a "less is more" approach usually works best. This means that you should put only one main thought or point on a single slide. Design-wise, keep your slides relatively simple and uncluttered. Don't feel the need to fill up the space on your slide and make it hard for the viewer to pick out what you want to highlight.

For remote presentations, make your slides even simpler and clearer than normal, with minimal text. Since in this case you can't direct your audience's attention to a certain place on the slide with your hand or a laser pointer, the audience will find it more of a challenge to focus on slides that are dense with information. Data-heavy slides in particular can cause your audience's attention to drift away from you and towards something more appealing.

Avoid the temptation to put large blocks of text on your slides, or lengthy bullet point lists. This only works when you go through the bullet point list slide-by-slide, meaning that you use a new slide to highlight each successive bullet point in the list, de-emphasizing the previous points as you go. Otherwise, you can alienate your audience very quickly with large chunks of text that appear on your slides at once. When you do this, you force the audience to have to read and also concentrate on you at the same time.

Minimize the number of font types you use on your slides, preferably using only one. Sans-serif fonts (like Helvetica) are easier to read when projected on a screen than serif fonts (like Times Roman), so I recommend that you stick with sans-serif for the most part.

Make sure the text on your slides is clearly visible and can be easily read without much effort, as your audience will get frustrated if they have to struggle to make out what you've written. Use a minimum font size of 32 points for your titles and 24 points for your body so that it will be easy for the audience to read. And ensure that your text is clearly visible and legible on whatever slide background you put it on.

Using slides in your presentation

You should be conscientious of not only how you design your slideshow, but also how you display it to the audience as you present.

Your main goal should be to integrate your slides into the presentation as smoothly and unobtrusively as possible. A small handheld slide advancing tool lets you change slides quickly and keeps your ideas flowing smoothly. Remember to keep this tool in your hand only when you are about to make a slide transition, and even then, try to practice advancing your slides without having to look down at it.

Switching between slides by clicking on a keyboard

takes up more time due to the need to hunt for the right key to advance the slides. You effectively have to take a small "technical break" every time you transition slides this way, which breaks up a smooth and efficient presentational flow.

You don't even need to break eye contact with the audience at all when you advance a slide, but can simply direct their attention to the new slide on the screen with your free hand to indicate the change. You will direct the audience's attention even more emphatically if you *do* break eye contact briefly to turn and face the screen, but don't turn your back to the audience when you do this. Use the arm closest to the screen to gesture at it, but hold the opposite shoulder in place, which will keep your front open and visible to those watching you.

For slides with complex information like charts, tables, or computer code, the audience will first need a moment to take in this information. When advancing to one of these slides, pause briefly and let them absorb the new information on it so that your words don't compete with the slide for their attention.

Always remain conscious of where your audience's line of sight is and how visible the screen is to them so that you don't accidentally block the screen with your body. If you feel your body is obstructing their view of the screen, feel free to ask, "Is everyone able to see the slides?" You'll most likely get an honest response to this.

Using multimedia elements in your slideshow

Just like your slides, integrate any audio or video in your presentation as smoothly as you can. Preparing beforehand is the best way to ensure this – cue up your files right before the presentation begins so that they are ready to start with just a few clicks.

If you have the opportunity, also test out your media files prior to the presentation to ensure that they work properly on the equipment they will be playing on. The audience will understand if you need a moment to launch your audio or video, but taking up too much time with this will make you look unprepared and less professional.

Technology will not always function in the way you want, however. If you present frequently, over time you will undoubtedly run into some or all of the following issues: your slides don't display properly on the projector you're using, they advance too quickly, pictures on certain slides have disappeared, special text fonts are missing or render differently, or you can't play an audio or video file.

But many of these problems will be apparent only to you, especially if you've forgotten to change or remove a slide from your slide deck. The audience may not be aware of the problem or may not have noticed it, so pay attention to how you react to it.

Several years ago, I watched a coworker of mine experience a minor technical glitch with her slideshow during a presentation. I don't remember now what the problem was, but what I do remember was her reaction to it: she visibly slumped her body, dropped her head, and gave a loud, frustrated sigh. Her reaction told me that "something really bad" had just happened. No matter what happens during your presentation, you don't want to put this thought into the audience's head.

Multimedia-related problems are admittedly harder to minimize or hide from the audience, as it is usually obvious to everyone that your audio or video isn't working properly. But when these problems inevitably crop up, handle them by remaining calm and collected and don't get visibly bothered by them.

When something goes wrong with multimedia, project an air of competent professionalism by demonstrating that you can either quickly fix whatever has gone wrong, or are otherwise able to move on in your presentation without the audio or video you had intended to show. Minimize the importance of the problem by showing that you have the ability to adapt to the new situation and keep going. This is actually good practice to follow no matter what problem you face during your presentation.

Presenting remotely

Presentations no longer have to be delivered with everyone in the same room anymore, as technology now allows us to deliver them to anyone on the globe. And you will certainly find yourself presenting over a phone line or to a webcam more often in the future. For some of my clients, the majority of their presentations are *already* delivered to audiences located far away from them.

What should we do differently when presenting remotely? First of all, keep in mind that remote presentations always require the use of some type of technology. Do you know how to use it? Do you know if it's working properly today? To answer a firm "yes" to both of the above questions, arrive earlier than normal at wherever you will be presenting and test that technology out. For remote situations, the entire success of your presentation can depend on whether the technology works or not.

Not long ago I was conducting a training session at a company that had recently installed cameras and monitors in all of their meeting rooms for video conferencing.

One of the participants suggested we use them to run our mock conference call activity, and although at this time I had only used their internal phone system, I agreed with the suggestion.

Unfortunately, the video conferencing system didn't work as I had expected, and although we got through it, we had a few glitches that created an awkward situation. This episode taught me never to spontaneously use any new technology without trying it out beforehand.

Also, take the time to test out the technical aspects of your presentation that you already know how to use. Another experience of mine illustrates this: the conference call code numbers I had been using for years at one company suddenly stopped working when I tried to use them in the middle of a workshop. I admit that it hadn't occurred to me that these codes might expire one day, and no one had warned me that this might happen. But I now test them out every time before the workshop begins to make sure they work, and avoid getting an unpleasant surprise in the middle of a session.

Since presenting remotely means that the audience is not in the same room as you, you will find it more of a challenge to make an emotional connection with them. If your presentation is voice only, it may help to visualize your audience in front of you and imagine yourself connecting with them as you would if they were there with you.

I also recommend that you stand when presenting remotely, even if the audience can't see you. Doing this will get you into your "presentational profile" and encourage the behaviors associated with it.

You should always start your presentation strong, with energy, dynamism, and confidence, but this is especially true for remote presentations, when we need to engage the audience right from the beginning. In general, try to maintain a high energy level throughout the presentation to prevent the audience from getting distracted or multitasking while you speak. You obviously can't stop them from doing this, but making your delivery as compelling as you can will work to limit any disengagement.

You can't make direct eye contact with the audience, so you need to make an effort to be more interactive than usual in your remote talks to compensate for this. For example, instead of stating a point outright, try to draw it from your audience. This technique works best if you can stimulate their curiosity in some way, or are fairly certain that at least some members of your audience will be able to provide an answer:

> *"Out of curiosity, can anyone guess what the average turnover rate is in this industry?"*

> *"What are some of the problems we've had recently with our suppliers? I know many of you are aware of this."*

You can also call on audience members directly by name to answer a question or offer their thoughts. Another option would be to show a menu of choices on a slide and ask your audience which ones they prefer. Think creatively and execute your ideas enthusiastically to encourage your audience to participate. They will appreciate your attempts to engage them in a remote setting.

If you are using a video camera as part of your remote presentation, look into it as you present. You will appear suspicious and disconnected to the audience if you let your eyes wander around the room while you speak. And be conscious of what is visible behind you to the audience. A bare wall, though bland, removes visual distractions and forces the audience to focus on you completely.

Finally, have a backup plan in place in case something goes awry, and know who to contact when it does. You'll be less likely to panic if you know in advance what steps you need to take and who can help you in the event of a technical failure.

RECAP:

- When you take questions from the audience, engage with the person through eye contact and remain engaged with them until you indicate you have completed your answer. Prepare for any tough questions you might receive, and maintain a professional and competent image if you don't know an answer.

- When you make slides for your presentation, remember that their function is either to complement your key points or help the audience understand and remember complex material. Don't put too much text on your slides, and integrate slides and any audio and video in your presentation as smoothly as you are able.

- For remote presentations, test out all equipment ahead of time. Be even more engaging and interactive than usual, and make sure you have a backup plan in place in case your technology doesn't do what you want it to.

CONCLUDING THOUGHTS

In this book, I've attempted to design a practical manual that anyone can use to create and deliver dynamic business presentations. As suggested by the title "Start to Finish," my intention was to give a comprehensive overview of the basics of presenting, starting from just an idea and covering a broad array of techniques and advice that have proven to work in many different situations.

We've covered how to find your presentation's purpose and message, craft an effective structure that supports that message, employ rhetorical tools to deliver your points, use your voice and body to communicate your ideas, and handle related issues like taking questions, using slides, and presenting remotely. While I can't claim that this information covers every single situation or topic related to business presentations, it provides enough knowledge to make your presentation a success, provided that you apply this knowledge.

Don't be too hard on yourself if you can't remember all the information in this book, or if you understand what to do in theory but find it a challenge to put it into practice during the presentation. Business presentations are frequently stressful, pressure-filled situations that most people try to get through the best they can, and despite their best intentions are unable to remember the tips they know they should be following.

Recognize that it will take time to become a powerful presenter, and be patient with yourself. Choose just a few pieces of advice from this book that you are not currently doing and resolve to try them out in your next presentation. When you've mastered those, choose a few more to try out for the presentation after that, and so on. Remember the importance of soliciting feedback from someone you trust who can be completely honest with you about your performance.

If there's one thing I want to make sure you remember from this book, even if you forget everything else, it would be this: no matter what else you do, *find a way to make a connection with every audience*. If you can do this successfully, your audience will usually be forgiving towards many other faults that you may have as a presenter, such as an unclear structure, a nervous appearance, or technical issues.

When you find a way to connect with your audience, you show that you understand what they want from you and your presentation. It makes them feel that their time with you was worthwhile, a good trade for their time and attention, and that you are a valuable employee or representative of your company. The audience feels that you made an effort to meet their needs, and it opens them up to your message.

Presentations have the power to influence people, give them useful knowledge, and form strong personal bonds. I wish you much success in your presenting endeavors.

ABOUT THE
AUTHOR

Steven D. Nelson is a business skills trainer who works with individuals and companies big and small to help them solve their communication-related needs. A presentation specialist, Steven has trained hundreds of businesspeople to become better presenters through workshops and coaching sessions. Steven is a native of Virginia Beach, Virginia, and is a graduate of Mary Washington College and Central European University. He lives with his family in Budapest, Hungary.

I invite you to join me by signing up at my website, stevendnelson.com, to get bonus material and discounts on future books. You can also send me your comments, concerns, omissions, or anything else, by writing to steven@stevendnelson.com.

www.ingramcontent.com/pod-product-compliance
Lightning Source LLC
Chambersburg PA
CBHW021446210526
45463CB00002B/646